HOW DO YOU BE A MAD SCIENTIST?

A BOOK FULL OF SCIENCE EXPERIMENTS

EGG

E=Mc2 ?

RADIOACTIVE
DANGER

written by
madeline j. hayes
illustrated by
srimalie bassani

SCIENTISTS ONLY BEYOND THIS POINT!

Sometimes the best way to learn is to just have fun and let curiosity be your guide. Have you ever wondered how to be a mad scientist? Do you wonder how people can make things explode and change color and grow and move? And not only HOW they do it but WHY it works? These are just some of the jobs of a mad scientist. Mad scientists are people who do scientific experiments that seem almost like magic. They are brave enough to try something new because they want to know what will happen. Mad scientists throughout history have been able to change the world by asking questions and solving problems!

Before attempting any of the experiments in this book be sure to get permission from a parent, guardian, or teacher!

RADIOACTIVE DANGER

Come along to learn some of the coolest experiments ever!
Share them with your friends and your family and discover
a world around you that's entirely mad and scientifically
amazing! Then you can go out and explore on your own!

goggles

lab coat

I highly recommend you put
on your best mad scientist
gear when performing these fun
experiments. Lab coats and goggles
are strongly encouraged!

gloves

HOW DO YOU MAKE YOUR OWN SLIME?

CHEMISTRY EXPERIMENT

SUPPLIES

1 container or bowl

1 cup
white washable glue

1 tsp
baking soda

2 Tbsp
contact lens saline solution

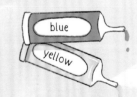

a few drops
of food coloring
(optional)

PROTOCOL

1. Add glue to your bowl.

2. If you are using food coloring, go ahead and add a few drops and mix it all together.

3. Add baking soda to the bowl and mix until combined.

4. Add contact lens saline solution and mix quickly.

5. Knead the mixture with your hands for a few minutes.

6. Enjoy your slime! Play around with it in your hands and observe what it feels like and how it moves on different surfaces.

WHY IT WORKS

Believe it or not, this simple experiment is all fueled by chemistry! When you combine the glue with the contact lens saline solution, a chemical reaction occurs and creates a polymer. A polymer is a type of substance made up of very large repeating molecules. In this experiment, the glue molecules cross link when they react with the contact lens saline solution and that forms your polymer (or slime)! The baking soda helps make it a little less gooey and a little firmer.

This is what we call a non-reversible chemical reaction, because it only goes in one direction. This means glue and contact lens saline solution can come together to make slime but you can't turn your slime back into glue and contact lens saline solution. An example of a reaction that is reversible is hydrogen and oxygen gas coming together to make water. You can reverse that chemical reaction and turn water into hydrogen and oxygen gas again.

glue + contact lens saline solution + food coloring (optional) = slime (polymer)

Try making slime with various amounts of the different ingredients and see how it changes the consistency. Exploring variables is a huge part of any good experiment!

As you play with your slime, do you notice anything? Slime feels like a liquid and a solid depending how you interact with it. If you let it slide around your fingers, it feels more like a liquid. If you hit it really hard, it feels more like a solid. This is due in part to the viscosity of the slime being affected by the amount of pressure you put on it.

Viscosity is a property of fluids that describes how easily the fluid slides around. Think about how water slides across the table easier than maple syrup. This is because they have different viscosities! Because slime's viscosity is different depending on how you apply pressure to it, it's called non-Newtonian fluid.

HOW DO YOU MAKE A BALLOON BLOW UP ON ITS OWN?

PHYSICS EXPERIMENT

SUPPLIES

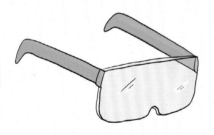

Eye protection or
safety goggles

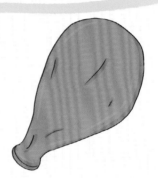

1 balloon

1 half-liter
plastic bottle filled half
way with dark soda

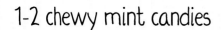

1-2 chewy mint candies

paper towels for clean up
(recommended)

Ask for permission first!

PROTOCOL

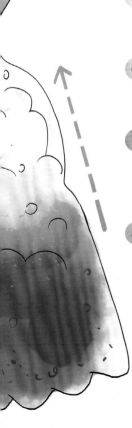

1. Choose your location. It is recommended you do this experiment outside because it can get messy.

2. Put on your eye protection.

3. Stretch out the balloon in different directions with your hands, being careful not to tear it. Set aside.

4. Remove the lid from the half-liter bottle and set it on the ground. Be sure to set it on flat ground and in an open area with nothing around or above it.

5. Take 1 or 2 candies and put them inside the balloon. Let them fall to the bottom. Hold the open end of the balloon up so they don't fall out.

6. Carefully place the open end of the balloon over the open end of the bottle without letting the candy fall in. Make sure the balloon is securely around the soda bottle so it will not fall off.

7. When you are ready, turn the balloon over so the candy falls quickly to the bottom of the bottle. Be careful not to let the balloon fall off and do not stand directly over the bottle in case the balloon pops and soda comes rushing out.

8. Once your balloon is full and the soda has settled in the bottle, you can carefully pinch the balloon above the bottle, pull it off, and tie it up!

Don't forget to clean up! All good scientists clean up their space when they're done so it's ready to go for the next experiment!

WHY IT WORKS

If your experiment worked correctly, your balloon should have blown up. Another option for this experiment is to skip the balloon and carefully drop the candy directly into the bottle. You'll see the soda come shooting up out of the top! (Only do this option if you're in a space where it is okay to spray soda everywhere.)

Why do these things happen? Soda has carbon dioxide gas trapped in it. That is what makes it taste bubbly and why it fizzes when you shake it up and open it. There is gas trapped inside the liquid. The bubbles you see in soda are carbon dioxide gas being released. When you drop the candy into the soda, it provides a surface area that aids the carbon dioxide in escaping the liquid holding it in.

This rapid release of gas pushes the liquid up until all the gas has escaped from the bottom where the candy is. The liquid falls back down into the bottle, but the gas floats on top because it has nowhere else to go. That gas is what fills the balloon.

Try this experiment out with different size soda bottles and different amounts of candy.

Be careful and do this with adult supervision because you might end up with a very strong explosion of soda.

HOW DO YOU MOVE PEPPER WITH SOAP?

HEALTH & PHYSICS EXPERIMENT

SUPPLIES

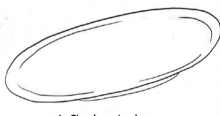

1 flat plate

1 cup water

1 Tbsp pepper

1 pump of soap

PROTOCOL

1. Set your plate on a flat surface.
2. Pour the water onto the plate.
3. Sprinkle the pepper all over the top of the water. (Most of it should stay floating on top.)
4. Put the soap on your pointer finger and dip your finger into the center of the plate with the water and pepper.
5. Watch as all the pepper shoots out to the edge of the plate.

WHY IT WORKS

Are you magic now? Can your touch make things move?
Yes, but your magic is science!

I am incredibly talented!

pepper

soap & water

Germs and pepper make me sneeze! Achooo!

When you touch the soap to the water's surface, it breaks the surface tension of the water. Water molecules want to interact with other water molecules. The soap disrupts the water molecules from interacting with each other so the water goes rushing as far away from the soap as it can get and brings the pepper along for the ride.

This is also a great illustration for how soap helps wash germs from your hands. The pepper is like the germs and the soap helps push them away from you so they go with the water down the sink when you wash your hands.

Noooo!

HOW DO YOU MAKE A BOUNCY EGG?

CHEMISTRY EXPERIMENT

SUPPLIES

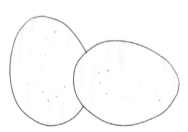

2 eggs

2 clear cups

3 cups water

3 cups white vinegar

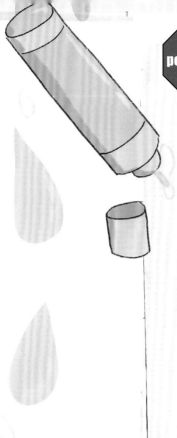

Ask for permission first!

PROTOCOL

1. Place an egg in each of the clear cups.

2. Cover one of the eggs with water.

3. Cover the other egg with white vinegar.

4. Check back during the first hour and watch bubbles start to appear on the surface of the vinegar-covered egg.

5. Check back in 24 hours and record your findings. Then again in 48 hours and do the same thing.

6. Take the eggs out of the cups and rinse with fresh water. Notice the differences between the two eggs.

vinegar

water

WHY IT WORKS

The egg in vinegar probably looks a little weird, shell-less, and bouncy, while the egg in water should look pretty much the same. What happened? It has to be the vinegar. But why? Vinegar is very acidic and the shell of the egg is basic. When acids and bases react with each other, they form new products such as carbon dioxide (CO_2 gas). Those are the bubbles you saw on the surface of the shell during your experiment. Water is a neutral liquid, meaning it is not an acid or a base. That is why it didn't interact with the base (the eggshell).

RESULTS

24 & 48 hours

vinegar

24 & 48 hours

water

Because the shell slowly dissolves off of the egg, you should be able to see the inside of the vinegar egg when you are done. Try bouncing it around!

Try placing eggs in different types of liquid to see what happens. Try acids like vinegar, soda, or even lemon juice!

HOW DO YOU MAKE ICE CREAM IN A BAG?

CHEMISTRY & FOOD SCIENCE EXPERIMENT

SUPPLIES

1 cup
milk

2 Tbsp
sugar

½ tsp
vanilla extract

3 or 4 cups
ice

½ cup
kosher salt

medium plastic
resealable bag

large plastic
resealable bag

toppings and a spoon
(optional)

PROTOCOL

1. Combine milk, sugar, and vanilla extract in the medium bag and seal tightly. Set aside.

2. Add ice and salt to the large plastic bag.

3. Put the medium bag with the milk mixture into the large bag with the ice and salt and seal the large bag.

4. Making sure both bags remain tightly sealed, gently shake the large bag for 3–5 minutes. You should feel the mixture cool down.

5. Periodically check the milk mixture until it is solid like ice cream.

6. Dig in and enjoy!

WHY IT WORKS

I scream, you scream, we all scream for ICE CREAM! And now you know how to make it anytime, anywhere with just a few simple ingredients! But how does it work?

The salt is the MVP of this experiment! When you take ice out of the freezer and leave it out at room temperature, it starts to melt on its surface. When you add salt to the ice, it disrupts the ice from refreezing on the surface by interacting with the surface of the ice cube, making it melt faster. The faster ice melts the more it pulls heat from its surroundings to use as energy in the melting process. In this experiment, heat gets pulled from the milk mixture, so while you are warming up the ice, you are cooling down the milk until it lightly freezes into ice cream.

HOW DO YOU MAKE COLORFUL FLOWERS?

BIOLOGY & NATURAL SCIENCE EXPERIMENT

SUPPLIES

daisies

carnations

4 white flowers
(carnations and daisies work best)

8 cups
water

4 different colors
of food coloring

4 different cups

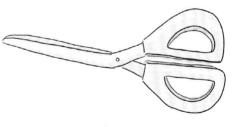

scissors

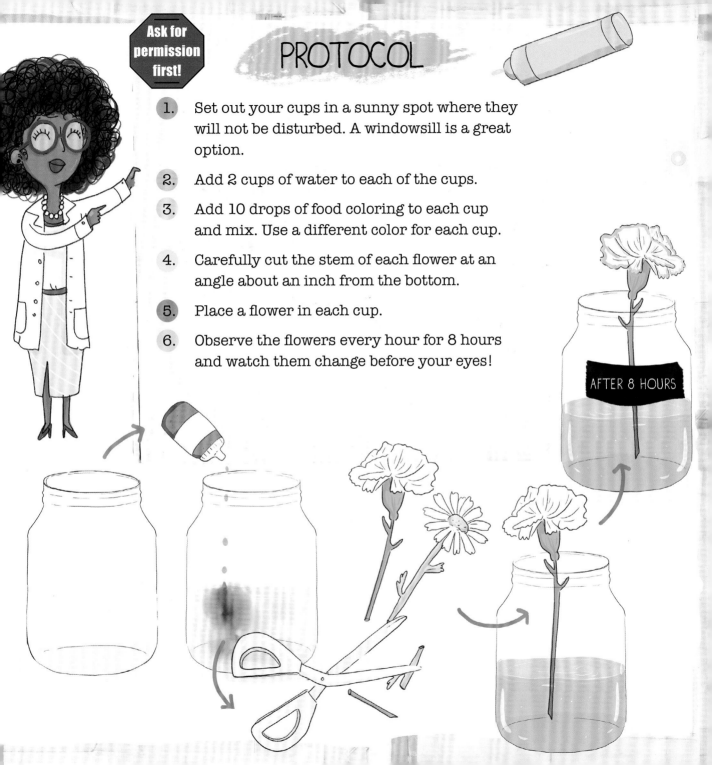

PROTOCOL

1. Set out your cups in a sunny spot where they will not be disturbed. A windowsill is a great option.

2. Add 2 cups of water to each of the cups.

3. Add 10 drops of food coloring to each cup and mix. Use a different color for each cup.

4. Carefully cut the stem of each flower at an angle about an inch from the bottom.

5. Place a flower in each cup.

6. Observe the flowers every hour for 8 hours and watch them change before your eyes!

AFTER 8 HOURS

WHY IT WORKS

This experiment is so fun to watch because of the pretty colors, but what you're seeing is how the water moves throughout a plant. The color helps you follow the movement over time. When the water moves up into the plant, you are watching a process known as capillary action.

If the flower still had roots, the water would start there. Then it would move up to the stem (which is where the water starts in this experiment), and finally up to the petals where you can start to see the color coming in.

Capillary action is when the water moves up the very tiny tubes in the stem (even though water doesn't usually move upwards on its own). Then the water evaporates off the petals and leaves in a process called transpiration. As the water transpires out, more water moves up the stem to replace it. The more water that moves up the more color that comes with it, so as time passes the flower slowly gets more and more colorful.

Try cutting the stem in two about halfway up and placing the stems in two different cups with two different colors!

FAMOUS "MAD" SCIENTISTS FROM HISTORY

Many scientists throughout history have interesting stories and have faced many obstacles when working to achieve their goals. Whether it was breaking boundaries or changing careers, these "mad" scientists made their mark!

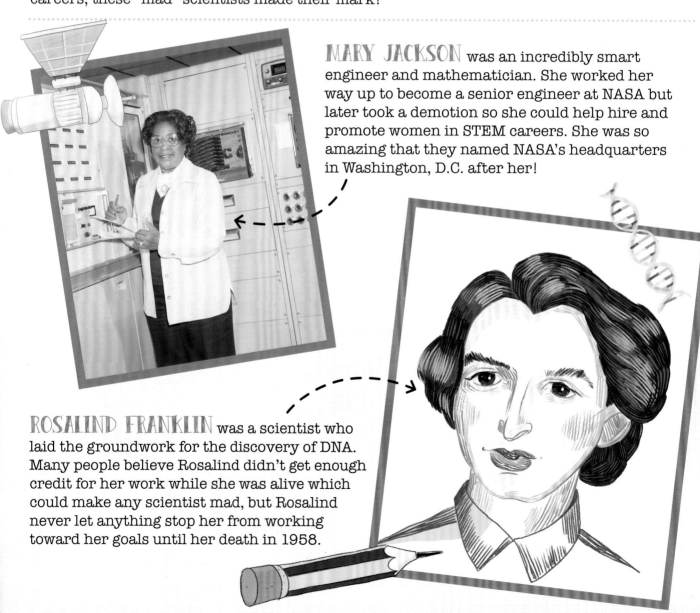

MARY JACKSON was an incredibly smart engineer and mathematician. She worked her way up to become a senior engineer at NASA but later took a demotion so she could help hire and promote women in STEM careers. She was so amazing that they named NASA's headquarters in Washington, D.C. after her!

ROSALIND FRANKLIN was a scientist who laid the groundwork for the discovery of DNA. Many people believe Rosalind didn't get enough credit for her work while she was alive which could make any scientist mad, but Rosalind never let anything stop her from working toward her goals until her death in 1958.

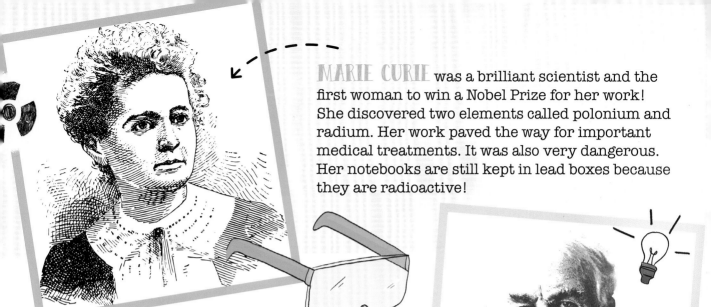

MARIE CURIE was a brilliant scientist and the first woman to win a Nobel Prize for her work! She discovered two elements called polonium and radium. Her work paved the way for important medical treatments. It was also very dangerous. Her notebooks are still kept in lead boxes because they are radioactive!

THOMAS EDISON, also known as the Wizard of Menlo Park, was a genius inventor. Like most scientists, he didn't always get it right on the first try. He said, "I have not failed; I've just found 10,000 ways that won't work." That's a lot of experiments! All of that work paid off in the end because he was able to invent many things we still use today, including the light bulb!

HEDY LAMARR was a glamorous actress, but she was also a self-taught inventor. Talk about a big career change! During World War II, she helped make a gadget for secret communication. Her invention helped make modern-day wireless communication possible!

HOW TO BECOME A ^(COOL) MAD SCIENTIST

Now that you have completed your first round of experiments, it's time to become a true mad scientist! Try out some of the ideas below!

GET A WACKY LAB COAT

You can't be a mad scientist without a lab coat! You can make your own by getting an oversized shirt with buttons. Decorate your lab coat with fabric markers, patches, buttons, pins, and anything else you can find!

CREATE YOUR MAD SCIENTIST LABORATORY

Set up a cool lab space in your room with lots of gadgets and gizmos. Old cereal boxes can become control panels, and toilet paper rolls can turn into telescopes.

COLLECT ODD INGREDIENTS

Search the house for weird ingredients like marshmallows, pickles, and rubber bands. You can even make up funny names for them, like "Marshmallowonium" or "Pickle plutonium."

INVENT A FUN CHARACTER

Every mad scientist needs an alter ego to become when they put on their disguise. Practice your catch phrase and go outside your box! It's all about having fun and being curious.

Remember, being a mad scientist is
all about having fun, being creative,
and using your imagination.

GIVE YOURSELF A MAD SCIENTIST NAME

Come up with a catchy name for your mad scientist alter ego. It could be
something like "Dr. Bubbles" or "Professor Fizzlewig." Try creating your own
by combining Dr. or Professor with a silly adjective and your favorite drink,
for example: "Dr. Comical Orange Juice."

TRY OUT SOME NEW EXPERIMENTS

Use whatever you can find to build a wild invention. Maybe it's a robot
that dances to your laughter or a time machine made
from a cardboard box. Let your creativity run wild!

SHARE YOUR MAD GENIUS

Invite your friends over for a "Mad Scientist Day" and
show off your laboratory and lab coat. Help them create
their own mad scientist name and share some of the
experiments you learned in this book.

GLOSSARY

Acid – a substance that has a pH less than 7 and can be used in chemical reactions; they tend to be sour and can be found in things like lemons

Base – a substance that has a pH greater than 7; it's the opposite of an acid and can neutralize it; it tends to be bitter and can be found in things like soap

Carbon Dioxide – a type of gas made up of carbon and oxygen atoms that we breathe out when we exhale; it's also what plants use for photosynthesis

Chemical Reaction – a process in which one or more substances change or combine to make different substances

Chemistry – the branch of science that studies the properties and behavior of different substances and how they can change or interact with each other

Experiment – scientists use experiments to make new discoveries, learn new things, and confirm their findings

Gas – a state of matter in which particles are spread out and move freely; oxygen is an example of a gas

Hydrogen – an element that is one of the building blocks of water

Liquid – a state of matter in which particles are close together but can still move around; water is an example of a liquid

Molecule – tiny particles that make up everything around us

Oxygen – an element that we breathe in to stay alive; it's also necessary for most living things to survive

Polymer – a type of material made up of long chains of tiny units

Saline Solution – a mixture made by dissolving salt in water

Scientist – a person who explores and discovers things by conducting experiments and asking questions to learn more about the world around us

Surface Tension – the "skin" that forms on the surface of a liquid because of the attraction between its molecules

Transpiration – the process in which plants release water vapor into the air through tiny openings in their leaves

Variable – something that can change or be changed in an experiment to see how it affects the outcome

Viscosity – a measure of how much something resists flowing; typically used to think about how thick or sticky a liquid is